GLOVEABLES

This edition published by Parragon Books Ltd in 2015
and distributed by

Parragon Inc.
440 Park Avenue South, 13th Floor
New York, NY 10016
www.parragon.com

Written, illustrated, and crafts made by Kate McCully
Designed by Claire Yeo   Edited by Kirsty Neale

ISBN 978-1-4723-6809-6

Printed in China

GLOVEABLES

PaRragon

Bath · New York · Cologne · Melbourne · Delhi
Hong Kong · Shenzhen · Singapore · Amsterdam

CONTENTS

WELCOME TO GLOVEABLES!

Let's face it: gloves and mittens are only really useful for several months of the year; the rest of the time they just take up space in closets and drawers. Give old gloves and mittens a new lease on life by turning them into a cute puppy or penguin friend—or something you can use all year round, such as a bag or a pincushion.

Gloves are great for mini projects because of their unique shape. The octopus in this book has glove fingers for legs, and the Stegosaurus has finger spikes! Multicolored gloves and chunky mittens will give your mini creations lots of personality, and buttons will make cute faces.

Once you get to grips with the projects in this book, you're sure to create your own collection of adorable gloveables. You might just need to buy new gloves and mittens for next winter!

Kate

*Sock lover, blogger, and
creator of Socktastic*

Tips and techniques

Stitching guides

If you need to draw guidelines for your stitches on a glove or mitten, the best thing to use is a felt-tip pen. Draw on the inside of the material, and press quite lightly so the lines don't show through on the outside. For white or very light-colored gloves, try using a pencil instead.

Cutting

You'll need to cut off parts of a glove or mitten to create different shapes or remove excess material. To do this, use a pair of small, sharp sewing scissors, and be careful not to cut too close to your stitches.

Stuffing

When stuffing your creations, it's best to add small pieces of toy filling at a time. Use the tip of your finger to push the filling into fiddly sections, such as arms, legs, and ears. You can buy toy filling in most craft shops.

Picture key

Each project has pictures as well as words to help you follow the steps. Cut where blue dotted lines are shown. Sew where red dotted lines are shown.

Skill levels

Each project gives you a difficulty rating:

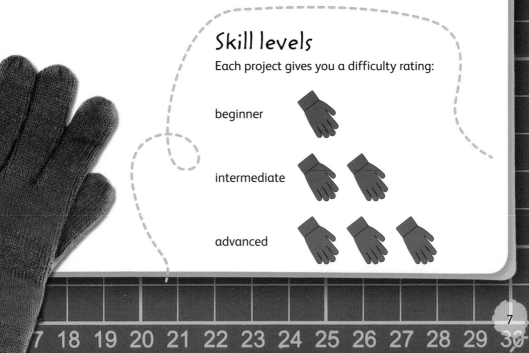

beginner

intermediate

advanced

SEWING TECHNIQUES

There are three main stitches you'll need to master in order to make the projects in this book: running stitch, backstitch, and ladder stitch.

Before you start sewing, tie a knot at the end of your thread. When you finish, make a few extra stitches to secure, then snip off the thread.

Keep stitches as small as you can, and use thread that is a similar color to the glove or mitten for a neat finish.

Running stitch: for general sewing

Pull your needle up through the material, then push it back down a short distance away to make the first stitch. Leave a gap, then make another stitch in the same way. Keep going to build up a line of neat and even stitches.

Backstitch: for creating shapes (such as arms, legs, and ears)

This stitch is especially secure, making it good for when you push toy filling up against it.

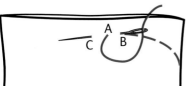

Pull your needle up through the layers of glove fabric (point A), then push it back down again a short distance away (point B) to make a single stitch. Bring the needle up through the glove again a short distance beyond point A to make another stitch (point C). Take it back down through the end of the previous stitch (A). Keep stitching in the same way, stitching back into the end of each previous stitch.

Ladder stitch: for joining stuffed pieces (such as arms, legs, and bodies)

This stitch helps you to join pieces invisibly.

Pin one piece (e.g. the arm or leg) to another (e.g. the body), tucking the rough edges inside.

Push the needle down through the first piece (e.g. the arm), then bring it up through the second piece (e.g. the body) and pull tight. Push it back down through the first piece and back up through the second, continuing in this way all around the edge you want to join.

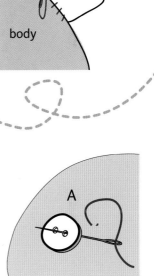

Sewing on buttons

Decide where you want the button to go, then push your needle into the glove or mitten at this point. Bring it straight back out a short distance away. Thread the needle up through one of the holes in the button (picture A).

Take the needle back down through the other buttonhole (picture B), and then in and out of the glove, as before.

Pull the thread so the button is flat against the glove. Repeat a few more times, going up through the glove and one buttonhole, and back down through the other until the button feels secure. Then tie a knot behind the button and snip off the excess thread.

If your button has four holes, sew through the other two in the same way.

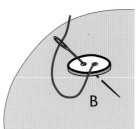

Gloves and mittens can be anything they want to be ...

OSWALD, THE GLOVE PUPPY

Oswald, the glove puppy, is lively and just a little naughty! He loves bumblebees, rock music, and running until his ears flap. Mini hot dogs are his favorite snack.

CHOOSE YOUR GLOVE:

tripy
attern

Pastel
color

YOU WILL NEED:

SKILL LEVEL

- 1 glove
- needle and thread
- scissors
- toy filling
- black embroidery thread
- large needle (for embroidery)
- 2 buttons

I'M READY TO PLAY!

13

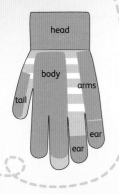

1. Making the body

Turn the glove inside out.

Draw on the shape of the body, as shown below, then sew along the lines using backstitch. Leave a ¾ inch gap for stuffing.

Sew a curved line at the end of the middle finger to make sure the legs are the same length.

Cut around the stitches, being careful not to cut into any other part of the glove yet.

Turn the body right side out, and stuff the legs with toy filling.

Sew a line across the top of the legs before stuffing the rest of the body.

2. Adding the head

Cut off the cuff at the end of the glove, just above the seam. You'll see it's made from two layers of material. Unfold it, making sure the material is inside out.

Draw on the shape of the head, as shown in the picture, then sew along the lines using backstitch. Leave a ¾ inch gap for stuffing.

Cut around the stitches, turn the head right side out, and stuff with toy filling.

Sew the head to the body using ladder stitch. Tuck the rough edges under as you sew.

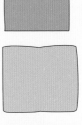

¾ in gap

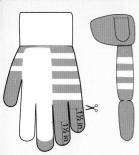

3. Creating the ears

Cut the last two fingers off your glove. They should each be about 1½ inches long.

Turn them right side out and sew to the sides of the head using ladder stitch.

4. Adding the arms

Cut two arm pieces from the side of the glove.

Draw on a curved shape for the arms, then sew along the lines using backstitch, leaving the short, straight ends open.

Cut around the stitches, turn each arm right side out, and stuff with toy filling.

Sew the arms to the sides of the body using ladder stitch.

5. Making the tail

Draw a tail shape onto the thumb of the glove, then sew along the lines using backstitch. Leave a ¾ inch gap for stuffing.

Cut around the stitches, turn the tail right side out, and stuff with toy filling.

Sew to the body using ladder stitch.

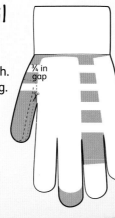

6. Creating the face

Sew on two buttons for the eyes.

Stitch a mouth and a triangle-shaped nose using black embroidery thread.

MARGO, THE HEDGEHOG PINCUSHION

Margo is a sensible hedgehog, who will take very good care of your pins! She's a brilliant tap dancer and enjoys a fruity smoothie at the end of a busy day. Her favorite flavor is banana.

CHOOSE YOUR MITTENS:

Dark brown

Pink or light brown

YOU WILL NEED:

SKILL LEVEL

- 1 dark brown mitten
- 1 light brown or pink mitten
- needle and thread
- scissors
- toy filling
- dry rice
- plastic wrap
- dark brown felt
- 2 buttons (for the eyes)
- 1 button (for the nose)

CAREFUL HOW YOU HUG ME!

1. Making the body

Turn the dark brown mitten inside out.

Measure about 2¾ inches down, and cut off the top.

Measure the width of the bottom of the cut-off section. Add ¼ inch to this measurement, and write the measurement down.

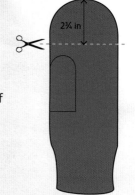

2¾ in

mitten width ⟷ plus ¼ in

2. Creating the base

Draw a circle onto brown felt, making sure it's the same diameter, or width, as the measurement you wrote down. Cut it out.

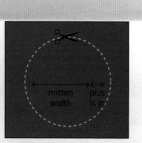

mitten width plus ¼ in

Sew the felt circle to the bottom of the body using backstitch. Leave a ¾ inch gap for stuffing.

¾ in gap

3. Stuffing the body

Turn the body right side out, and stuff with toy filling.

Fill until it's almost (but not quite) full.

18

4. Adding the rice

Wrap a big handful of rice in two layers of plastic wrap, then pat it down to make a round disk.

Push the disk of rice into the bottom of the body (this will give weight to the pincushion).

Sew the hole shut using ladder stitch.

5. Making the head

Turn the light brown or pink mitten inside out.

Cut along one side of the mitten to make two layers of material.

Draw on the shape of the head, as shown in the picture.
Sew along the lines using backstitch.

Cut around the stitches, turn the head right side out, and stuff with toy filling.

Sew the head to the body using ladder stitch.
Tuck the rough edges under as you sew.

6. Adding the finishing touches

Sew on two buttons for the eyes.

Sew on another button for the nose.

Finally, add your pins!

WE'RE SO GLOVEABLE!

MILES, THE STEGOSAURUS

Miles is kind and funny, and he has very good manners for a dinosaur. He likes derby hats and playing badminton on weekends. He also enjoys coloring, but he's not very good at staying inside the lines.

CHOOSE YOUR GLOVES:

Fingerless

Patterned

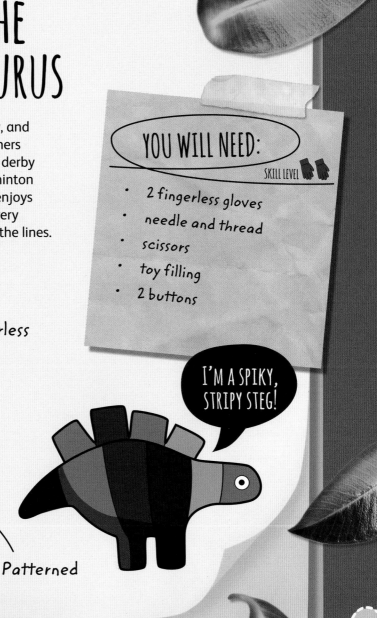

YOU WILL NEED:

SKILL LEVEL

- 2 fingerless gloves
- needle and thread
- scissors
- toy filling
- 2 buttons

I'M A SPIKY, STRIPY STEG!

1. Making the spikes

Turn the first glove inside out.

Cut off the fingers, leaving about ¼ inch underneath, so they all stay joined together.

Sew across the top of each finger using backstitch. Turn right side out.

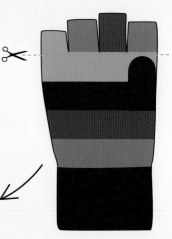

2. Making the body

Turn the second glove inside out.

Sew across the bottom of the thumb, then cut it off.

Cut along the side of the glove to make two layers of material.

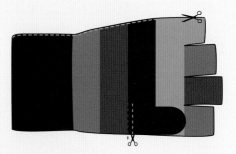

3. Adding in the spikes

Draw on the shape of the body,
as shown in the picture.

Then pin the spikes between the two
layers of the body, curving the edge to
match the curve of the back, as shown.

Sew all the way around the body using
backstitch. Leave a ¾ inch gap for stuffing.

Note: Make sure you sew through the edge of the spikes as you go.

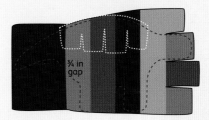

¾ in
gap

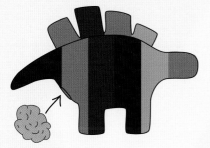

4. Stuffing

Turn the body right side out,
and stuff with toy filling.

Sew the hole shut using ladder stitch.

5. Adding the finishing touches

Sew on two buttons for the eyes—
one on each side of the head.

DRAWSTRING BAG

Carry your favorite goodies wherever you go with this supersmart bag. Pick a pretty pair of mittens and add some fluffy pom-poms to make it look even cuter. Easy as pie!

CHOOSE YOUR MITTENS:

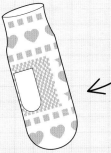

→ A pair

Colorful pattern

YOU WILL NEED:

SKILL LEVEL

- 2 mittens
- needle and thread
- scissors
- chunky knitting yarn
- large needle
- 2 pom-poms

1. Creating the bag

Cut along the side of each mitten. Then open each mitten out to make two big pieces of material.

Turn the thumbs inside out.

Sew across the bottom of each thumb, then cut each one off.

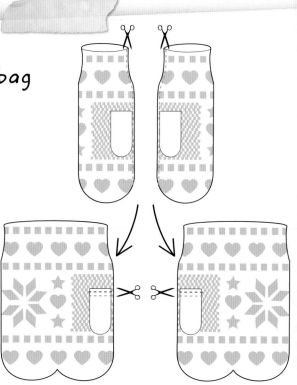

2. Sewing the bag together

Pin the two pieces of material together, with the right sides facing.

Sew along three sides using backstitch. Leave the top edge open.

3. Making the drawstring

Turn the bag right side out.

Thread the large needle with a piece of chunky knitting yarn.

Starting at the center front, sew a line of big running stitches all the way around the top edge of the bag.

Leave about 4 inches of yarn hanging down at each end of the stitching.

4. Adding the finishing touches

Thread the large needle again with one of the yarn ends.

Push the needle through the middle of a pom-pom.

Slide the needle off, and tie a knot in the end of the yarn.

Add a pom-pom to the other yarn end in the same way.

PERCY, THE OCTOPUS

Percy is a little chatterbox.
He loves thunderstorms,
peppermint candies, and
playing pranks on his friends.
He also gives really good hugs.

CHOOSE YOUR GLOVES:

A pair

LET'S SHAKE
HANDS ... ALL
OF THEM!

Smart
stripes

1. Making the body

Turn both gloves inside out.

On each one, draw on a curved line to make the body, as shown in the picture, then cut along the lines.

Cut just one of the two curved pieces off from each glove, snipping in a curved line, just above the fingers.

You should have one tall layer and one short layer on each glove.

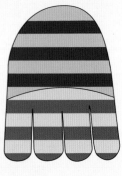

2. Making the legs

Sew a curved line at the end of the three longest fingers to make sure the legs are the same length.

Snip off the excess material, close to the stitching.

Do the same to the other glove.

3. Sewing the body together

Pin the two body pieces together, with the short pieces on the inside.

Sew around the curved side edges and the section between the fingers using backstitch. Leave a ¾ inch gap for stuffing.

¾ in gap

4. Stuffing

Turn the octopus right side out, and stuff with toy filling.

Sew the hole shut using ladder stitch.

5. Adding the finishing touches

Sew on two buttons for the eyes.

Try using a big white one with a small colored one on top.

STRAWBERRY DECORATION

Who could resist this cute strawberry? It's easy to make from just one mitten! Use the ribbon to hang it up in your bedroom, or clip it to your school bag instead.

CHOOSE YOUR MITTEN:

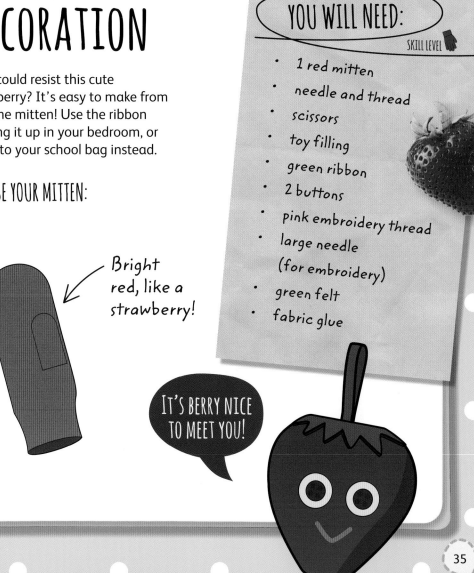

Bright red, like a strawberry!

YOU WILL NEED:

SKILL LEVEL

- 1 red mitten
- needle and thread
- scissors
- toy filling
- green ribbon
- 2 buttons
- pink embroidery thread
- large needle (for embroidery)
- green felt
- fabric glue

IT'S BERRY NICE TO MEET YOU!

1. Cutting the shape

Turn the mitten inside out.

Draw on a stawberry shape, as shown in the picture, then cut it out.

You should have two identical strawberry-shaped pieces.

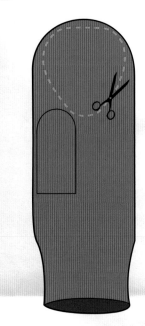

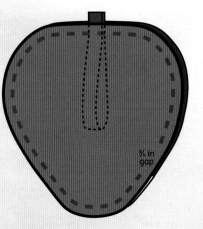

¾ in gap

2. Adding in the ribbon

Fold a piece of green ribbon in half.

Pin it between the two layers of the strawberry, as shown.

Sew all the way around the strawberry using backstitch. Leave a ¾ inch gap for stuffing.

Note: Make sure you sew through the ends of the ribbon as you go.

3. Stuffing

Turn the strawberry right side out, and stuff with toy filling.

Sew the hole shut using ladder stitch.

4. Creating the leafy top

Draw a leaf shape onto green felt. Cut it out.

Stick the felt leaf to the top of the strawberry using fabric glue.

Note: Push the ribbon through the hole.

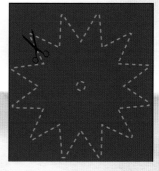

5. Adding the finishing touches

Sew on two buttons for the eyes.

Stitch a smiley mouth using pink embroidery thread.

ERNEST, THE PENGUIN

Ernest is the coolest penguin you'll ever meet! He's a champion snowball-thrower with a surprisingly good singing voice. He collects snow globes and likes to read adventure stories.

CHOOSE YOUR MITTENS:

Mittens

Black or gray

CHILL OUT, DUDE!

1. Making the body

Turn the first mitten inside out.

Tip: Lay it flat and make sure the thumb is right at the edge.

Draw on a curved line to make the top of the head, as shown in the picture.

Tip: Use chalk to mark lines on the glove.

Sew along the line using backstitch, then cut off the excess material.

Cut straight across the curved end of the mitten.

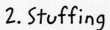

2. Stuffing

Turn the body right side out, and stuff with toy filling.

You don't need to stuff the thumb.

3. Sewing the body shut

Thread the needle with two strands of thread.

Sew a line of big running stitches all the way around the bottom of the mitten.

When you get back to where you started, gently pull the thread ends to close the hole.

Push the rough edges of the mitten inside. Hold the thread tightly in one hand, and make a few extra stitches to keep the hole firmly closed.

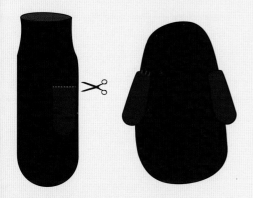

4. Creating the second wing

Cut the thumb off the second mitten.

Sew the thumb to the other side of the body using ladder stitch. Tuck the rough edges under as you sew.

5. Adding the finishing touches

Draw a triangle onto orange felt. Cut it out to make the beak.

Draw a rounded rectangle onto white felt. Cut it out to make the tummy.

Stick the felt in place using fabric glue.

Sew on two buttons for the eyes.

WHAT A GLOVELY PAIR!

Ernest and Emily

BIBI, THE BUNNY

Bibi is a sweet little bunny with big dreams. She loves cozy blankets and is learning to play the harmonica. Her favorite flowers are daisies and sunflowers.

CHOOSE YOUR GLOVE:

Pink is fun!

Plain or patterned

YOU WILL NEED:

SKILL LEVEL

- 1 glove
- needle and thread
- scissors
- toy filling
- 2 small black beads
- pink embroidery thread
- large needle (for embroidery)
- 1 small white pom-pom

I GLOVE YOU!

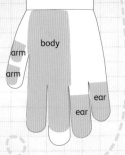

1. Making the body

Turn the glove inside out.

Draw on the shape of the body, as shown in the picture, then cut along the lines.

Sew a curved line at the end of the middle finger to make sure the legs are the same length.

2. Adding in the ears

Cut the last two fingers off your glove, making sure they're the same length, then turn them right side out.

Pin them between the two layers of the body, at an angle, as shown.

Sew all the way around the body using backstitch. Leave a ¾ inch gap for stuffing.

Note: Make sure you sew through the ends of the ears as you go.

¾ in gap

equal equal

3. Stuffing the body

Turn the body right side out, and stuff with toy filling.

Sew the hole shut using ladder stitch.

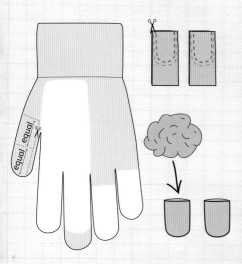

4. Adding the arms

Cut two arm pieces from the thumb of the glove.

Draw on a curved shape for the arms, then sew along the lines using backstitch, leaving the short, straight ends open.

Cut around the stitches, turn each arm right side out, and stuff with toy filling.

Sew the arms to the sides of the body using ladder stitch. Tuck the rough edges under as you sew.

5. Adding the finishing touches

Sew on two beads for the eyes.

Stitch a mouth and a triangle-shaped nose using pink embroidery thread.

Sew a white pom-pom to the back of the body to make the tail.

MAKE YOUR CREATION FAMOUS!

Send a pic of your creation to *imadeit@parragon.com* and we'll share
your photo online using hashtag **#Gloveables!** **@ParragonBooks**

Please don't include yourself in the photo, we want to see your creation! By sending us a photo
of your creation, you agree to the terms and conditions stated here: www.parragon.com/imadeit